YOUNG PEOPLES LIBRARY SERVICE

310.1

Mother Teresa
Saint of the Slums

Nina Morgan

WAYLAND

Title page: Mother Teresa with some Indian children in October 1979.

Editor: Carron Brown
Designer: Joyce Chester
Production controller: Carol Titchener

First published in 1998 by Wayland Publishers Limited, 61 Western Road, Hove, East Sussex BN3 1JD

Find Wayland on the Internet at
http://www.wayland.co.uk

British Library Cataloguing in Publication Data
Morgan, Nina
Mother Teresa: Saint of the Slums. — (Famous Lives)
    1. Teresa, Mother, 1910–1997 – Juvenile literature
    2. Missionaries of Charity – Juvenile literature
    3. Women missionaries – India – Biography – Juvenile literature
    I. Title
266.2'092
ISBN 0 7502 2289 1

Typeset in England by Joyce Chester.
Printed and bound in Italy by G. Canale & C.S.p.A.

Picture Acknowledgements
The publishers would like to thank the following for allowing their pictures to be reproduced in this publication: AKG, London 4; All Action *cover*, 30; Associated Press 14; Bridgeman Art Library 7; BBC Photo Library 27; Camera Press 22, 35, 39, 43 (bottom), 45; Croatian Catholic Mission 5, 9, 11, 12 (left), 13; Getty Images 15; Robert Harding 10; Impact 19 (both), 26; Popperfoto 17, 29, 33, 34, 40; Rex Features, London 16, 21, 23, 28, 31, 32, 38, 41; Frank Spooner 36, 37; Sygma 1, 18, 44; Topham Picturepoint 20, 24, 42; Trip 6, 8, 12 (right), 43 (top).

While every effort has been made to secure permission, in some cases it has proved impossible to trace copyright holders.

Contents

Growing Up

In the small town of Skopje in Albania, Agnes Gonxha lived with her parents Nikolle and Drana, her brother, Lazar, and her sister, Age, in a large house with a big garden. Agnes was the youngest. She was always called Gonxha (which means flower bud) by her family because she was pink and plump and cheerful.

Her parents always gave a warm welcome to any person in need who came to their house. The Bojaxhiu family never turned away anyone who needed help. This was a lesson that Agnes, who grew up to be Mother Teresa, never forgot.

The busy market place in Skopje in 1918.

Agnes was only eight years old when her father died, but her mother worked hard to make sure that her children's days were happy ones.

Religion played an important part in their lives. 'My mother taught us to love God and to love our neighbour,' Agnes remembered.

'We lived for each other and we made every effort to make one another happy. We were a united and very happy family.' Mother Teresa, recalling her childhood.

When she was fourteen, Agnes (sitting) posed for this photograph with her brother, Lazar, and her sister, Age.

Devout Catholics

The Bojaxhiu family were Roman Catholics. Like other Christians, Catholics believe that God came to the world through His Son, Jesus Christ. As well as praying to God and Christ, Catholics also pray to the Virgin Mary, the mother of Jesus, and to saints, very holy people who they believe now look down on earth from heaven.

Local priests play the most important part in the day-to-day religious lives of many Catholics.

'We lived next to the parish church of the Sacred Heart of Jesus. Sometimes my mother and sisters seemed to live as much in the church as they did at home. They were always involved with the choir, the religious services and missionary topics.'
Mother Teresa's brother, Lazar Bojaxhiu.

The headquarters of the Catholic Church is in Rome, Italy. The head of the Catholic Church is the Pope. But for the Bojaxhiu family, as for most Catholics, it was their local priest who played the most important part in their daily lives.

Agnes and her sister took part in many church activities. Agnes loved to read about missionaries and the lives of the saints. She began to dream about becoming a missionary in India.

This is a painting of Pope Benedict XV, who was Pope from 1914 to 1922, during the time that Agnes was growing up.

Answering a Call

When Agnes was 12 years old, she believed that she heard God calling to her, asking her to become a nun.

Some Catholic women recognize that they have a calling, to join a religious community and become a nun. When they become nuns they take solemn vows to obey and serve God.

'Put your hand in His [God's] hand and walk all the way with Him.'
Drana Bojaxhiu's advice to her daughter Agnes.

The decision to become a nun is a very serious one. Catholic nuns devote their lives to serving God. They believe Christ to be their husband, so they promise never to marry and have children. They also take solemn vows of poverty and obedience. This means that they promise to live very simply with few possessions and to obey the rules of their religious communities without question.

Agnes told her mother about her feelings. They prayed together to the Virgin Mary for help in deciding the right thing to do. Agnes also asked the local priest for help. In the end, Agnes believed she heard the Virgin Mary advising her to follow God's call.

When she was ten years old, Agnes (left) posed with some of her friends in Skopje.

The Irish Ladies

Below: *The Loreto Abbey in Ireland. Agnes travelled here in 1928 to learn English and begin her life as a Loreto nun. She was just eighteen when she arrived.*

Agnes had to wait for six years before she was old enough to join a religious order. During that time she read about the work of missionaries working in India. 'They used to give us the most beautiful descriptions of the experiences they had,' she recalled. Agnes came to believe that God was calling her to work in India.

Right: *After she left for Ireland, Agnes never saw her mother again. She left her this picture to remember her by.*

She also learned about the Loreto nuns, or the 'Irish ladies', who were an international order of nuns founded in the sixteenth century. The Loreto nuns set up schools in India and many other countries.

When Agnes was 18 years old, she applied to join the Loreto order in India. But first she had to travel to the Loreto Abbey in Ireland to learn English. As she boarded the train for Ireland, she said goodbye to her mother for the last time. She never saw her again.

Teaching in India

After just two months in Ireland, Agnes was sent to the Loreto House in Darjeeling, India, to begin her novitiate – the first step towards taking final vows as a nun. For the next two years, she learned to live as a nun. She also studied English and Bengali, one of the Indian languages.

Left: *Sister Teresa (left) with another novice at the Loreto convent in Darjeeling, in 1929.*

Above: *St Thérèse of Lisieux. Agnes adopted her name when she became a nun.*

Sister Teresa (top right) with four other Loreto nuns in the Loreto convent in Calcutta, India. Sister Teresa had just taken her final vows as a nun, and was appointed principal, or head teacher, of St Mary's School.

When she was 21 years old, Agnes took her first vows and adopted the religious name of Teresa. 'Not the big St Teresa of Avila, but the little one,' she explained. By the 'little one' she meant Thérèse of Lisieux, a French nun who believed in the 'little way' – working for good by carrying out very simple tasks joyfully.

The new Sister Teresa was sent to teach geography and history at St Mary's, a Loreto School in Calcutta. She loved her work. In 1937, she became headteacher of the school and took her final vows as a Loreto nun.

'I was the happiest nun at Loreto. I dedicated myself to teaching.'
Sister Teresa describing her life as a Loreto nun.

A Call Within a Call

But after seventeen happy years in the Loreto order, Sister Teresa's life changed very suddenly on 10 September 1946 – a day she remembered as her 'Day of Inspiration'.

Sister Teresa's second calling from God came when she was quietly praying on a train travelling from Calcutta to Darjeeling. She recalled, 'The message was very clear. I had to leave the convent and consecrate [devote] myself to helping the poor by living among them. It was a command. I knew where I had to go, but I did not know how to get there.'

'Prayer is in all things,' believed Mother Teresa. She urged her followers to 'pray lovingly like children'.

Although she was sure that God was calling her to work among the poor, Sister Teresa was very sad at the thought of leaving the Loreto order.

'*I knew that God wanted something from me.*'
Sister Teresa describing how she was called to serve the poorest of the poor.

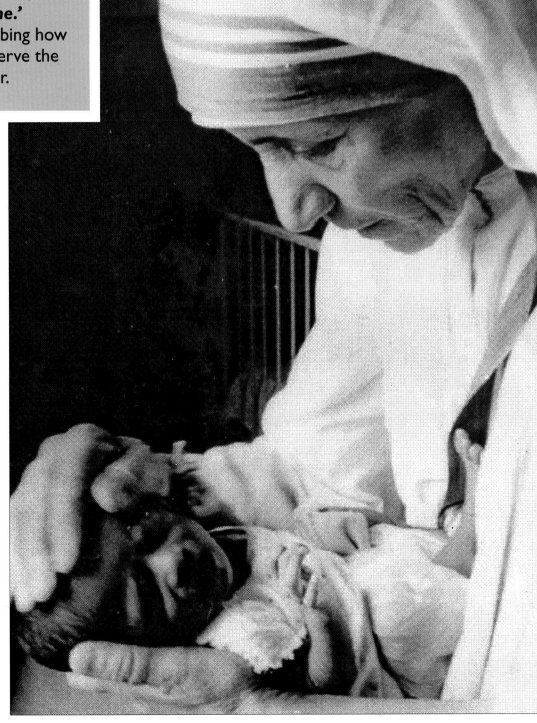

Mother Teresa believed all children were a gift from God. She set up many homes to look after sick, orphaned and unwanted children.

A New Life

Leaving the Loreto nuns was hard. She had to get special permission from her own order and from the Pope to live as a nun outside the convent.

Sister Teresa changed her nun's habit for a cotton sari,
which became her uniform for the rest of her life.

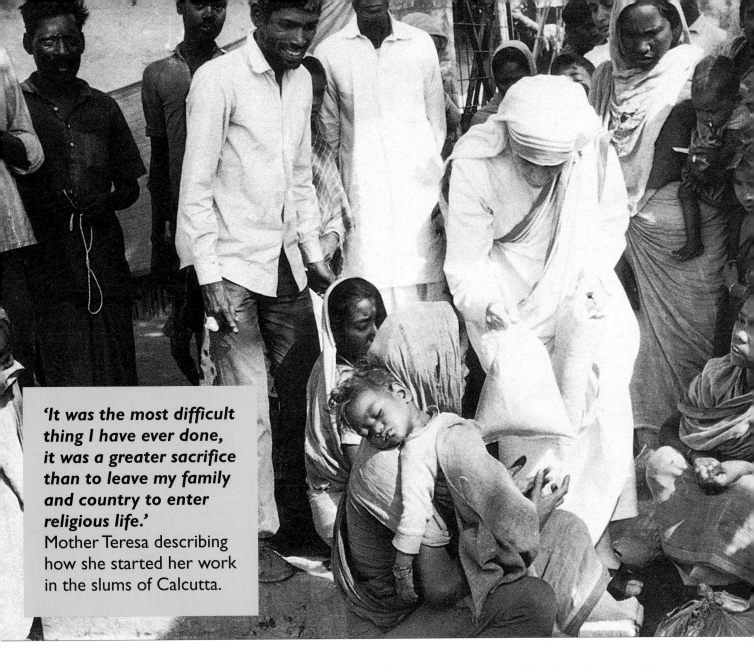

'It was the most difficult thing I have ever done, it was a greater sacrifice than to leave my family and country to enter religious life.'
Mother Teresa describing how she started her work in the slums of Calcutta.

Sister Teresa finally left the Loreto convent in Calcutta on 16 August 1948. When she went she put on a white cotton sari like those worn by poor women in India. The sari had a blue border to remind her of the Virgin Mary. On her left shoulder she pinned a cross. She wore this uniform for the rest of her life.

On 20 December 1948, after a short course in nursing, Sister Teresa went out for the first time by herself to work in the slums of Calcutta. She had just 5 rupees in her pocket. She began by starting a school on the street.

Mother Teresa gives out Christmas presents of rice and blankets to the poor of Calcutta.

Life in the Slums

Mother Teresa walking through the slums, or bustees, of Calcutta.

Calcutta is the fourth largest city in the world, and for many people it is the heart of India. It is also one of the world's most crowded cities.

Many people in Calcutta lead comfortable lives, but there are many others who are so poor that they have to live on the streets. Peaceful and rich neighbourhoods exist side by side with terrible slums.

'We lived surrounded by a sea of poverty and suffering. Nevertheless this sea can decrease in size. Our work is only a drop in the bucket, but this drop is necessary.' Mother Teresa.

In the slums, Sister Teresa saw that the luckier people made their homes under old sacks – others had no homes at all. Many were dressed only in rags. Hunger and disease were everywhere.

She found old or sick people left on the streets to die, eaten by rats and insects. Unwanted babies were thrown on to rubbish heaps. The disgusting smells of rotting garbage and sickness came as a great shock to Sister Teresa.

Below: *A slum area along one of the canals in Calcutta. The slums here are among the worst in the world.*

Right: *A slum child in Calcutta picking over rubbish, hoping to find something he can use.*

A New Order

Sister Teresa found her new work very hard and very lonely. 'Today, my God, what tortures of loneliness,' she wrote in her diary. 'Tears rolled and rolled.' But she was convinced she was doing what God wanted.

Soon she was joined by other women who wanted to help the poor of Calcutta. On 7 October 1950, the Pope gave Sister Teresa permission to set up a new order of nuns, the Missionaries of Charity. As head of the new order, Sister Teresa became known as Mother Teresa.

Prayer plays a very important part in the lives of the Missionaries of Charity. 'We should be professionals in prayer,' urged Mother Teresa. 'If we want to be able to love, we must pray!'

'To be able to love the poor and know the poor we must be poor ourselves.'
Mother Teresa.

In addition to their vows of poverty, chastity and obedience, the Missionaries of Charity added a new vow: 'to give wholehearted, free service to the very poorest'.

They lead a very simple life. Each nun owns only three saris, a pair of sandals, underwear, a crucifix, a bucket to wash in, and a prayer book. They wake before 5 a.m. to pray, before going out to work in the slums.

Many young women became members of the Missionaries of Charity because they wanted to join Mother Teresa in her work.

A Home for the Dying Poor

Every day in the slums of Calcutta Mother Teresa came across destitutes – very poor people – who were dying in the streets alone. She was determined to help them to die in peace with respect.

In 1952, she set up Nirmal Hriday (meaning the Home of the Pure Heart) in a Hindu temple in Calcutta. When the Missionaries of Charity found people dying on the streets, they brought them to Nirmal Hriday to care for them and show them that they were loved by someone.

Mother Teresa and the Missionaries of Charity helped the poor in many ways. In Calcutta they arranged for food to be collected, cooked and given to poor people every day.

In 1953, as more and more women came to join them, the Missionaries of Charity moved to a bigger house at 54 Lower Circular Road in Calcutta. This is still their headquarters, or Motherhouse, today. Later, ordinary men and women began to help her order.

Mother Teresa and the Missionaries of Charity set up Homes for the Dying to offer comfort and love to very sick people dying alone on the streets.

'I've lived like an animal on the street, but I'm going to die like an angel, loved and cared for!' A man picked up from the gutter by the Missionaries of Charity.

Serving the Poorest of the Poor

Nirmal Hriday was just the start. Mother Teresa wanted to help the poor to live as well as to die. The Missionaries opened more schools, rescued unwanted babies and set up homes for abandoned or orphaned slum children. They also set up centres to help people who suffered from leprosy, a terrible disease that deforms their bodies.

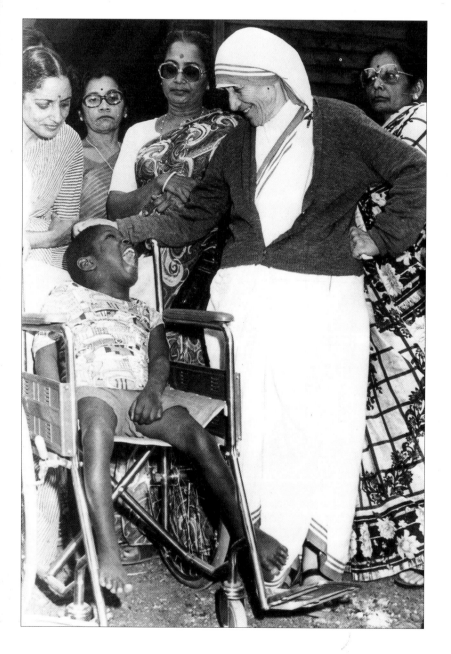

In 1965, Mother Teresa opened the first house to help the poor outside India, in Venezuela. More houses quickly followed. Today, the Missionaries of Charity and their co-workers run more than 450 centres in over 100 countries to help the poor.

The Missionaries of Charity now run centres, like this shelter for disabled people in Nairobi, Kenya, to help the poor in many countries around the world. Mother Teresa visited them all.

Setting up and running the centres costs money. Where does it come from? Mother Teresa believed that in some way God would provide the money for her to carry out her work. And she has been proved right. Many people all over the world pay for the work by giving money without being asked.

Even in rich countries, poor people still need help. In 1986, Mother Teresa opened her first centre to help the poor in Chicago, Illinois, USA.

'I am like a little pencil in God's hand. He does the thinking. He does the writing. The pencil has only to be allowed to be used.'
Mother Teresa on her role.

Something Beautiful for God

For nineteen years the Missionaries of Charity helped thousands of poor people, but most ordinary people had never heard of them. This changed suddenly in 1969 when the British journalist Malcolm Muggeridge and a BBC television crew made a film about Mother Teresa and her work. They called the film 'Something Beautiful for God'.

The film made Mother Teresa famous all over the world. Donations poured in and many people felt that Mother Teresa's example changed their lives. One of these was Malcolm Muggeridge himself.

The journalist Malcolm Muggeridge made a film about Mother Teresa, and believed that meeting her changed his life.

In 1968 Malcolm Muggeridge interviewed Mother Teresa for his documentary film 'Meeting Points'. In this scene from the film she is shown talking to a young Indian doctor.

He believed that his cameramen recorded an actual miracle taking place when they were filming in the house for the dying. No one expected the scenes filmed in such dark rooms would come out, but when the film was processed everyone was amazed to find that those scenes were bathed in a beautiful soft light.

Fame Spreads

After the film was shown, prizes and praise began to flood in from around the world. Mother Teresa was awarded honorary degrees from several universities, including Harvard University in the USA, Cambridge University in Britain and Dublin City University in Ireland. She was also given many awards. She immediately spent any prize money on the poor.

The president of Dublin City University echoed the feelings of many when he said 'Mother Teresa's spirituality and achievements challenge us to analyse many of the values and attitudes that exist in our society.'

In 1979, Mother Teresa was awarded one of the most famous prizes of all: the Nobel Peace Prize.

In 1979, Mother Teresa was awarded the Nobel Peace Prize. When she heard the news she replied: 'I accept this award in the name of the poor'. She then asked the organizers to cancel the celebration dinner and give her the money they would have spent so that she could spend it on the poor.

'Mother Teresa has personally succeeded in bridging the gulf that exists between rich nations and poor nations.' The 1979 Nobel Prize Committee.

As the world recognized her work, awards continued to flood in. The year before she died Mother Teresa was granted honorary American citizenship. Just four others had been awarded this honour in the 222-year history of the USA.

The Most Powerful Woman in the World

Some people believed Mother Teresa became 'the most powerful woman in the world' because when she asked to see or speak to presidents and prime ministers around the world, she was often put straight through.

World leaders answered Mother Teresa's calls because they realized that she did not seek attention for herself or her order, but for the problems concerning the poor. She touched the hearts of the toughest leaders in the world.

Prince Charles visited Mother Teresa's homes for the poor in Calcutta several times. He admired her and felt great respect for her work.

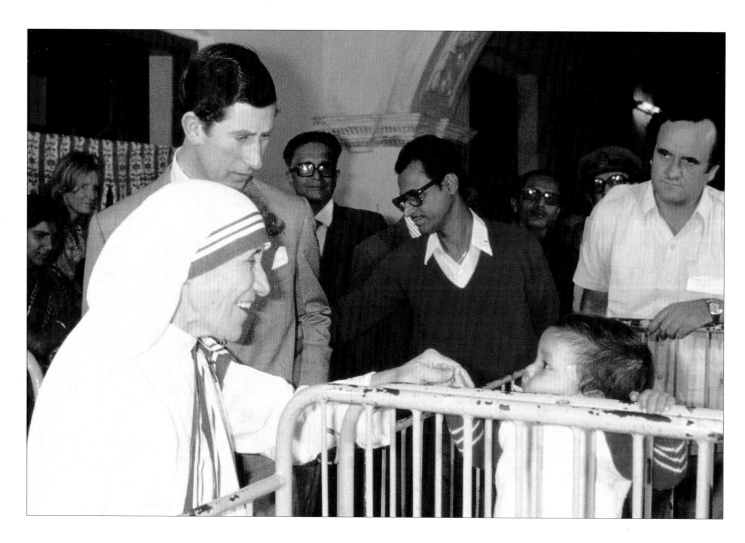

US President Bill Clinton and his wife Hillary were proud to welcome Mother Teresa on a visit to the USA. While she was there, Mother Teresa was taken by Mrs Clinton to see a maternity ward in a hospital in Washington DC.

[She was] 'the most outrageous, manipulative and brilliant PR performer I have ever seen.'
Rock star and charity worker, Bob Geldof, speaking of his admiration for Mother Teresa.

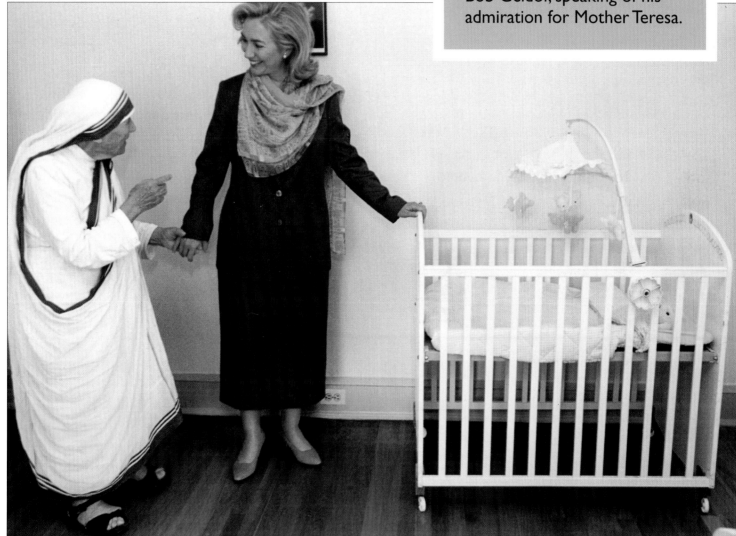

Mother Teresa was not afraid to use her power. In 1988, she urged the British government to do something to help homeless people living on the streets of London. The prime minister at the time, Margaret Thatcher, promised to take action. But a year later, when Mother Teresa saw no homes for the homeless had been built, she spoke out against the government's lack of action.

Spreading the Word

A phone call from Mother Teresa could sometimes result in immediate action. During the Ethiopian famine in 1981, Mother Teresa felt inspired to write to US President Reagan. He quickly phoned to promise to do everything possible to provide help. He was as good as his word. The US government rushed in with food and medicine.

US President Clinton was another admirer. When Mother Teresa visited the United States he felt honoured to receive her. President Clinton replied to a speech she gave calling for peace and celebration of life by saying she had 'truly lived'.

US President Ronald Reagan, shown here with his wife Nancy, was one of many world leaders who answered Mother Teresa's calls for help.

Diana, Princess of Wales, agreed with him. She met Mother Teresa in 1992. In her own way, Diana worked to help Mother Teresa. She also hoped to show her sons, the Princes William and Harry, the work done by the Missionaries of Charity in the Calcutta slums.

'If she tells them how important it is to make their families strong, they will listen. If she asks them to care for the poor, for the homeless, they will hear her.'
Mother Teresa describing Diana, Princess of Wales.

Diana, Princess of Wales, became a great friend and admirer of Mother Teresa. Like many people around the world, Mother Teresa was saddened by Diana's death, just a few days before her own.

Blessed are the Poor

Mother Teresa did not think it at all strange that she should be called to work with the poorest of the poor. She believed it was the best way to answer God's call and show her deep love for God. 'The work we do [with the poor] is nothing more than a means of transforming our love for Christ into something concrete,' she said.

Poor people of all religions are welcomed and helped at the Missionaries of Charity Mission in Calcutta, India.

The poor, she felt, are very special people because they can teach others a lot about what really matters in life. 'Our sisters and brothers work for the very poorest of the poor – the sick, the dying, the lepers, the abandoned children,' she wrote. 'But I can tell you that in all these years I have never heard the poor grumble or curse, nor have I seen any of them dejected with sadness.'

'The poor do not need our compassion or our pity; they need our help. What they give to us is more than what we give to them.' Mother Teresa.

'Know the poorest of the poor among your neighbours,' said Mother Teresa. When she was helping the poor Mother Teresa believed she was being given a wonderful chance to do 'something beautiful for God'.

Love Until it Hurts

Love played a very important part in Mother Teresa's life. She was inspired by Jesus' words 'Love one another, as I have loved you'. Her work was driven by her great love for God and she urged people to 'love until it hurts'.

'If you don't want a child,' said Mother Teresa, 'give it to me.' In their orphanages and children's homes, Mother Teresa and the Missionaries of Charity looked after children whom nobody wanted.

'Being unwanted is the worst disease that any human being can ever experience.' Mother Teresa.

'Let us always meet each other with a smile,' she often said, 'for a smile is the beginning of love.'

Mother Teresa believed it was important for every person, however poor or rejected, to know that someone loved them, even if it was only during the last few minutes of their lives. She opened her homes for the dying poor so that they could die in dignity, surrounded by peace and love.

'Poverty is even greater when it is a poverty of the heart,' she said. 'I want you to find the poor here, right in your own home first. And begin love there.'

The Missionaries of Charity also opened shelters to help disabled people.

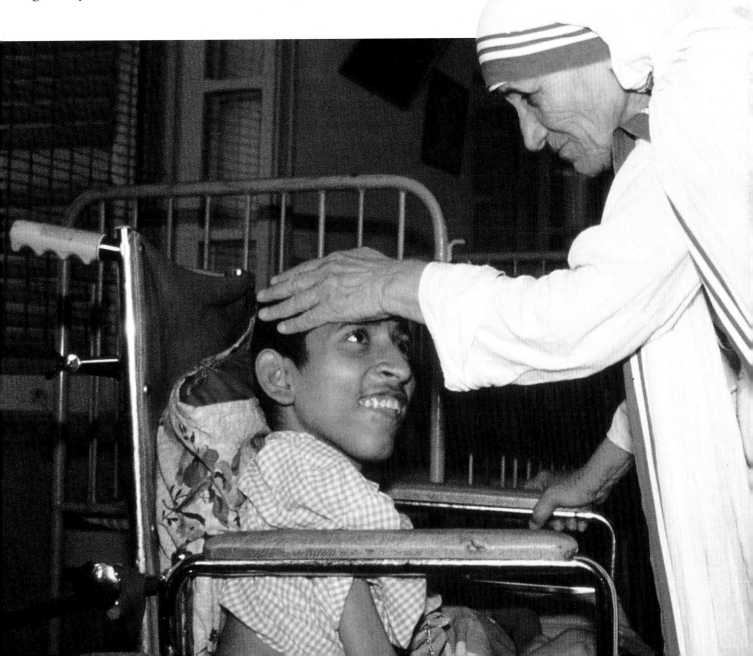

Something in Common

Although Mother Teresa was a Catholic nun, she had great respect for other religions because she believed that all people need to experience God's love in their own way.

Some missionary groups hope to convert people to their own beliefs through the work they do. This was not the aim of Mother Teresa or the Missionaries of Charity.

'Every human being comes from the hand of God, and we all know something of God's love for us.'
Mother Teresa.

'Our lives are centred on prayer,' said Mother Teresa. The Missionaries of Charity begin each day at 5.30 a.m. with prayers, and all day long they continue to pray by 'making their work a prayer'.

Mother Teresa had great respect for all religions and often visited churches and temples devoted to other religions. In this Sikh temple in India she thanked the worshippers for their gifts of books, flowers and money to help in her work with the poor.

She was even happy to help people who did not believe in any God at all. But, admitted Mother Teresa, 'I do convert. I convert you to be a better Hindu, a better Catholic, Muslim, Jain or Buddhist.'

To people of all religions in Calcutta she was simply known as Mother. 'We cannot view her through Catholic eyes, or Hindu eyes, but only through human eyes, for she does not discriminate,' said Michael Gomes, whose family provided the first home for the Missionaries of Charity.

Saying Goodbye

When Mother Teresa was nearly 80 years old, she began to suffer from heart trouble. In 1990, she decided to resign as the head of the Missionaries of Charity because of her poor health. But she agreed to stay on when the Missionaries insisted they could not find anyone to take her place.

Although she became increasingly weak, Mother Teresa continued to travel and to work at the Home for the Destitute and Dying in Calcutta. But finally, in March 1997, she became too frail to carry on. She died at the Motherhouse of a heart attack on 5 September 1997.

Soldiers carried Mother Teresa's coffin during the long procession to her final resting place at the Motherhouse of the Missionaries of Charity. Many world leaders and ordinary people came to the funeral to say a final goodbye to Mother Teresa.

Nearly half a million people of all religions came to say a final goodbye. She was buried near the Motherhouse chapel. On her grave are carved the words of Jesus Christ, 'Love one another as I have loved you'.

'How can I be [afraid of dying] when I have watched and been with so many who have died? No, on the contrary, I look forward to it.'
Mother Teresa.

After Mother Teresa died, the courtyards at the houses run by the Missionaries of Charity were beautifully decorated with flowers brought by ordinary people who wanted to show their respect and love for Mother Teresa.

The Future

When Mother Teresa retired in March 1997, Sister Nirmala, a 63-year-old sister in the Missionaries of Charity, was chosen to take over as the head of the order. Sister Nirmala was born a Hindu and later became a Catholic.

Although she now leads the order, Sister Nirmala refuses to take on the title Mother. Such a title is, she explains, 'not due to me'. She faces a very difficult task. Mother Teresa was a very unusual person because she could gain attention and support from both ordinary people and important world leaders for her cause of helping the poor. Her personality and holiness caught the imagination of millions.

When Mother Teresa (right) became too weak to carry on as head of the Missionaries of Charity, Sister Nirmala (left) was elected to take her place.

'Just as God found me, He will find someone else.' Mother Teresa.

It will, admits Sister Nirmala, be difficult for her to work in the same way. 'No one can ever replace Mother Teresa,' she says. But she and the other Missionaries of Charity vow to continue to serve the poorest of the poor.

Right and below: *In the Home for Dying Destitutes in Calcutta, the Missionaries of Charity continue to provide love, food and shelter for the poor. Sister Nirmala and the Missionaries of Charity are determined that their work will continue.*

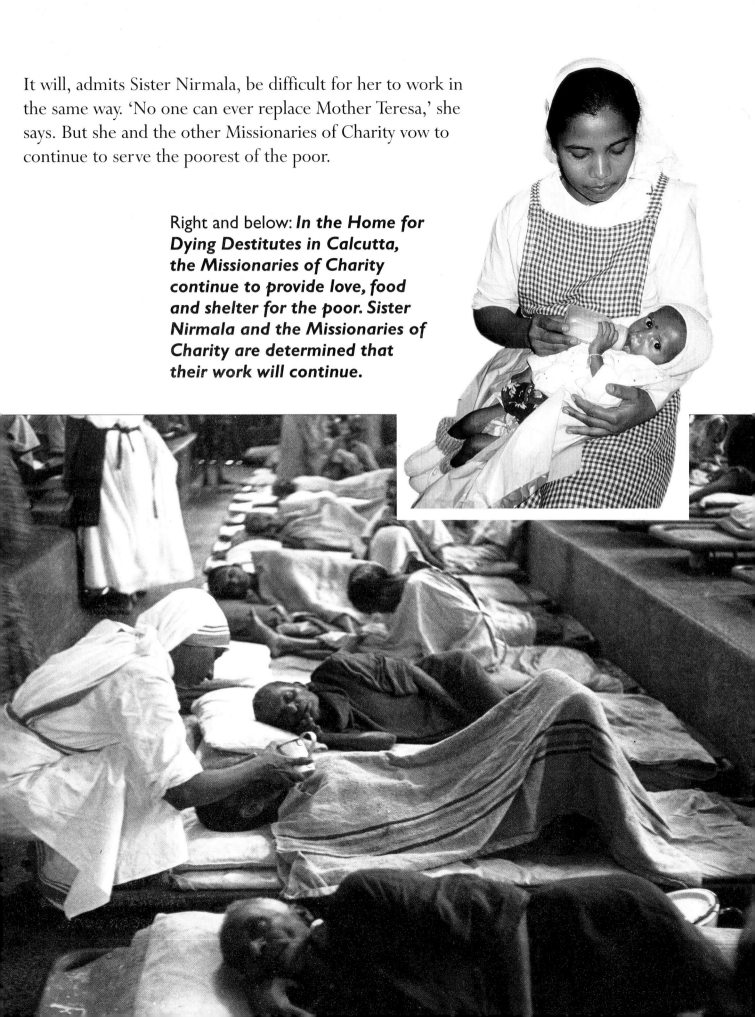

Is She a Saint?

For many people, Mother Teresa was a powerful force for good. But not everyone believes that Mother Teresa carried out her mission in the best way.

Some disagreed with her ideas. Others criticized her for accepting money to help the poor from anyone, even criminals. Some said she should have run the homes for the dying and poor differently. Others complained that she ruled the Missionaries of Charity with too strong a hand.

No one knows whether the Catholic Church will officially declare her to be a saint. But no matter what, millions of people are grateful for the difference Mother Teresa made to their lives.

For many people, both rich and poor, Mother Teresa was a saint on earth.

'It will be for posterity to decide whether she is a saint,' says Malcolm Muggeridge. 'I only say of her that in a dark time she is a burning and a shining light … in a godless time, the Word dwelling among us, full of grace and truth.'

Mother Teresa often quoted the words from the Bible: 'Unless you become like a little child, you cannot enter into heaven.'

'Even her bitterest critics cannot deny that she changed the world that she was born into … and she did indeed accomplish something beautiful for God.'
Journalist Mary Kenny writing in *The Independent*.

Glossary

Abandoned Left alone.

Abbey The headquarters of a group of nuns or monks.

Boarded Got on.

Chastity To agree not to get married or have children.

Convert To encourage someone to change their beliefs.

Crucifix A religious symbol in the form of a cross.

Dedicate To give all one's time and energy to something.

Deforms Eats away or makes bent or broken.

Dejected Discouraged or depressed.

Devote To give all your time to.

Discriminate To treat some people differently from others.

Famine A situation in which there is no food, so people starve to death.

Frail Weak.

Hindu Hindus worship several gods. Hinduism is the main religion in India.

Manipulative Able to convince people to do what you want.

Missionaries Religious people who go to live in poor countries where they try to help local people and teach them about their religion.

Orphaned A child whose parents have died.

Poverty To be poor.

PR Public relations. A PR person works to bring things to people's notice.

Religious order A group of men or women who devote their lives to serving God. Men belonging to a religious order are known as brothers, or monks; women are called sisters, or nuns.

Resign To step down.

Rupees The unit of money used in India. One rupee is not worth very much.

Sari A type of long dress worn by women in India.

Slums Very poor and run down areas of a city.

Solemn Very serious.

Spirituality Belief in God.

The Word The messages of Christ.

Vows Solemn and serious promises.

Date Chart

1910, 16 August Agnes Bojaxhiu is born in Skopje, Albania.

1928, 26 September Agnes leaves Skopje to join the Loreto nuns in Ireland.

1931, 24 May Agnes makes her temporary vows and takes on religious name, Teresa.

1931 Teresa is sent to the Loreto convent in Calcutta.

1937 Teresa takes her final vows; becomes headteacher at St Mary's.

1946, 10 September The 'day of inspiration' when Sister Teresa hears God calling her to serve the poor.

1948 Leaves the Loreto convent to work in the slums of Calcutta.

1950, 7 October Receives permission from the Pope to set up a new order of nuns: the Missionaries of Charity.

1952, 22 August Opens the first home for dying poor, Nirmal Hriday, in Calcutta.

1953 The Missionaries of Charity move to their Motherhouse in Calcutta.

1965 The Missionaries of Charity set up their first home outside India, in Venezuela.

1969 The film 'Something Beautiful for God' makes Mother Teresa famous around the world.

1979 Mother Teresa accepts the Nobel Peace Prize 'in the name of the poor'.

1990 Mother Teresa retires as the head of the Missionaries of Charity due to poor health. Later that year she agrees to stay on.

1997, 17 March Mother Teresa steps down a second time because of poor health.

1997, 5 September Mother Teresa dies.

Further Information

Books to Read

Gray, Charlotte, adapted by Susan Ullstein, *Mother Teresa: Servant to the World's Suffering People* (Gareth Stevens Inc., 1990)

Gray, Charlotte, *People Who Have Helped the World: Mother Teresa* (Exley Publications Ltd, 1991)

Jackman, Wayne, *Life Stories: Mother Teresa* (Wayland, 1993)

Moore, Rosemary, *Famous Lives: Campaigners for Change* (Wayland, 1997)

Tames, Richard, *Mother Teresa* (Franklin Watts, 1990)

Audio tapes:

A simple path (Mother Teresa talking about her philosophy and work, 180 minutes), available from Talking Tapes Direct, PO 190, Peterborough, PE2 6UW, UK.

Index

All numbers in **bold** refer to pictures as well as text.